PRAYING FOR OTHERS

QUOTATIONS FROM THE WRITINGS OF ELLEN G. WHITE

PACIFIC PRESS PUBLISHING ASSOCIATION

NAMPA, IDAHO

OSHAWA, ONTARIO, CANADA

Edited by Jerry D. Thomas
Designed by Linda Griffith
Cover photo by Mark Lisk

White, Ellen Gould Harmon, 1827-1915
    Praying for others : quotations from the writings of Ellen G. White /
[compiled by Ken and Debby Wade].
      p.   cm.
    ISBN 0-8163-1405-5 (alk. paper)
    1. Intercessory prayer—Quotations, maxims, etc. 2. Seventh-day
Adventists—Doctrines—Quotations, maxims, etc. 3. White, Ellen Gould
Harmon, 1827-1915—Quotations. I. Wade, Kenneth R., 1951-. II. Wade,
Debby, 1951-. III. Title.
BX6154.W45924 1997
248.3'2—dc21   97-24843
                                                      CIP

97 98 99 00 01 • 5 4 3 2 1

INTRODUCTION

How often have our hearts been cheered, our spirits uplifted, our courage strengthened by the simple words "I'll be praying for you!" And yet how easy it is to say those words with good intentions and then to go on our way and forget our promise.

Ellen G. White was a woman of prayer. In her early Christian experience she reported long seasons of prayer, laboring and pleading for the souls of her young friends, some of whom were careless and flippant. But she kept on praying until every one of them was converted.

Based on her own experience, and the light that God gave her, she often encouraged Christians to pray for one another, for the sick, and for those who had not yet accepted Christ. Here, gathered from her collected writings, are short quotations that will instruct and encourage you as you uplift others in prayer. It is our prayer that these words will be a blessing to you and through you the blessing will pass to many more.

—The Compilers

Ωf you are a child of God, your prayers,
and your work to strengthen and build up
will have an influence,
and God will bestow His blessing upon you.
PC 172

*L*et us work upon this plan, and pray for one another,
bringing one another
right into the presence of God by living faith.
RH 28 August 1888

*J*esus prayed! The majesty of Heaven prayed!
He wept in behalf of man.
Prayer, faithful, earnest prayer
will move the arm that moves the world.
ST 15 January 1880

*B*egin to pray for souls;
come near to Christ, close to His bleeding side.
Let a meek and quiet spirit adorn your lives,
and let your earnest, broken, humble petitions
ascend to Him for wisdom that you may have success
in saving not only your own soul,
but the souls of others.
1T 513

*W*ith all our treatments given to the sick,
simple fervent prayer should be offered
for the blessing of healing.
We are to point the sick to the compassionate Saviour,
and His power to forgive and to heal.
3SM 296

Souls are to be sought for, prayed for, labored for.
Earnest appeals are to be made.
Fervent prayers are to be offered.
Our tame, spiritless petitions
are to be changed into petitions of intense earnestness.
7T 12

*T*hose who engage in house-to-house labor
will find opportunities for ministry in many lines.
They should pray for the sick
and should do all in their power
to relieve them from suffering.
6T 83, 84

*B*e always kind and courteous,
cheerful and hopeful.
Keep praying and working for souls.
6MR 379

All that can be done in praying for the sick
is earnestly to importune God in their behalf,
and in perfect confidence rest the matter in his hands. . . .
If the life of the sick can glorify him,
we pray that they may live; nevertheless,
not as we will, but as He wills.

HL 239

*W*e sent up our humble petitions
for the sick and afflicted one,
who was losing his hold on this life.
As we presented this case before the Lord,
we felt the assurance of the love of God
even in this affliction.
RH 11 October 1887

As we seek to win others to Christ,
bearing the burden of souls in our prayers,
our own hearts will throb
with the quickening influence of God's grace;
our own affections will glow with more divine fervor;
our whole Christian life will be more of a reality,
more earnest, more prayerful.
COL 354

$\mathcal{B}$efore we were blessed with institutions
where the sick could get help from suffering,
by diligent treatment and earnest prayer in faith to God,
we carried the most seemingly hopeless cases
through successfully.
Today the Lord invites the suffering ones
to have faith in Him.
Man's necessity is God's opportunity.
3SM 295, 296

Oh, that the earnest prayer of faith
may arise everywhere,
Give me souls buried now in the rubbish of error,
or I die!
Bring them to the knowledge of the truth
as it is in Jesus.
TDG 171

*W*hen self dies,
there will be awakened an intense desire
for the salvation of others,—
a desire which will lead to persevering efforts to do good.
There will be a sowing beside all waters;
and earnest supplication, importunate prayers,
will enter heaven in behalf of perishing souls.
GW 470

Christ wrestled in earnest prayer;
he offered up his supplications to the Father
with strong crying and tears in behalf of those
for whose salvation he had left heaven,
and had come to this earth.
Then how proper, yea,
how essential that men should pray and not faint!
RH 1 April 1890

would come before the Lord with this petition:
"Lord, we cannot read the heart of this sick one,
but thou knowest whether it is for the good of his soul
and for the glory of thy name to raise him to health.
In thy great goodness, compassionate this case,
and let healthy action take place in the system.
The work must be entirely thine own."
HL 239

We anointed the child and prayed over it,
believing that the Lord
would give both mother and child peace.
It was done.
The cries of the child ceased,
and we left them doing well.
2SG 110, 111

*L*et those who are spiritual
converse with these souls.
Pray with and for them.
Let much time be spent in prayer
and close searching of the word.
Let all obtain the real facts of faith
in their own souls through belief that
the Holy Spirit will be imparted to them
because they have a real hungering
and thirsting after righteousness.
6T 65

*L*et the voice of prayer be heard
in our institutions in behalf of the sick,
that they may place themselves where they can cooperate
with Him who can save both soul and body.
6MR 379

*H*umble workers,
who do not trust in their own strength,
but who labor in simplicity, trusting always in God,
will share in the joy of the Saviour.
Their perservering prayers will bring souls to the cross.
7T 27

But after I have prayed earnestly for the sick, what then?
Do I cease to do all I can for their recovery?—
No, I work all the more earnestly,
with much prayer that the Lord may bless the means
which his own hand has provided;
that he may give sanctified wisdom to co-operate with him
in the recovery of the sick.

HL 240

We should pray to God much more than we do.
There is great strength and blessing
in praying together in our families,
with and for our children.
CG 525

$\mathscr{T}$he desire to be a blessing
discovers the weakness and inefficiency of the worker.
This drives the soul to God in prayer,
and the Lord Jesus gives light and His Holy Spirit,
and they understand that it is Christ
who does the melting and breaking of the hard hearts.

Ev 466

*W*e shall be called upon to make
most decided efforts to extend the work of God,
and prayer to our heavenly Father will be most essential.
It will be necessary to engage in prayer in the closet,
in the family, and in the church.
Our households must be set in order,
and earnest efforts must be made to interest
every member of the family in missionary enterprises.
RH 4 July 1893

Prayer, short, weighted with tenderest sympathy,
presenting the suffering one in faith to the Great Physician,
will inspire in them a confidence, a rest,
and a trust that will tend to the health
of both soul and body.

GosHealth 1 June 1897

*W*here the way is clear
for the offering up of prayer for the sick,
the case should be committed to the Lord in calm faith,
not with a storm of excitement.
He alone is acquainted with the past life of the individual,
and knows what his future will be.
HL 238

Among God's people there should be at this time
frequent seasons of sincere, earnest prayer.
The mind should constantly be in a prayerful attitude.
In the home and in the church
let earnest prayers be offered in behalf of those
who have given themselves to the preaching of the Word.

HP 87

I entreat you who fear the Lord
to waste no time in unprofitable talk
or in needless labor to gratify pride
or to indulge the appetite.
Let the time thus gained
be spent in wrestling with God for your ministers.
Hold up their hands
as did Aaron and Hur the hands of Moses.
5T 162

In the word of God
we have instruction relative to special prayer
for the recovery of the sick.
But the offering of such prayer is a most solemn act,
and should not be entered upon
without careful consideration.

MH 227

2—P.O.

$\mathcal{L}$et those older in experience
watch over the younger ones;
and when they see them tempted,
take them aside, and pray with them and for them.
MYP 18

If the members of the churches would but put to work
the powers of mind that they have, in well-directed efforts,
in well-matured plans, they might do a hundredfold more
for Christ than they are now doing.
If they went forth with earnest prayer,
with meekness and lowliness of heart,
seeking personally to impart to others
the knowledge of salvation,
the message might reach the inhabitants of the earth.
RH 11 April 1893

$\mathcal{T}$he spirit of intercession came upon me,
and I was drawn out in most earnest prayer
for souls at Battle Creek. I know their peril.
The Holy Spirit has in a special manner
moved me to send up my petitions in their behalf.
TM 63

We are to come to God in faith,
and pour out our supplications before Him,
believing that He will work in our behalf,
and in the behalf of those we are seeking to save.
We are to devote more time to earnest prayer.
3BC 1146, 1147

When we have prayed for the recovery of the sick,
whatever the outcome of the case,
let us not lose faith in God.
MH 233

$\mathcal{O}$ur faith can be just as firm, and more reliable,
by committing the desire to the all-wise God,
and without feverish anxiety, in perfect confidence,
trusting all to him. . . .
Our petitions must not take the form of a command,
but of intercession for him
to do the thing we desire of him.
HL 239

There is to be the greatest freedom in their conversation,
speaking one to the other in reference to the truth,
the labors and prayers in behalf of the souls ready to die.
Tell the story of the interest that angels have in the salvation
of the human souls for whom Christ has given His life.
21MR 294

Earnest prayer was offered to God,
and hearts were softened and subdued
by the influence of the Spirit of God.
Their prayers were uttered with freshness and power.
As the word of God was explained,
I saw that a soft, radiant light illumined the Scriptures.

9T 35

Satan is enraged at the sound of fervent prayer,
for he knows that he will suffer loss.
1T 295

No human power can save the sick,
but, through the prayer of faith,
the Mighty Healer has fulfilled His promise
to those who have called upon His name.

3SM 36

$\mathcal{L}$et Christ find you His helping hand
to carry out His purposes.
By prayer you may gain an experience
that will make your ministry
for your children a perfect success.
CG 69

We should hold convocations for prayer,
asking the Lord to open the way
for the truth to enter the strongholds
where Satan has set up his throne,
and dispel the shadow
he has cast athwart the pathway
of those whom he is seeking to deceive and destroy.
6T 80

*W*atch continually to cut off the current,
and roll back the weight of evil
Satan is pressing in upon your children.
The children cannot do this of themselves.
Parents can do much.
By earnest prayer and living faith,
great victories will be gained.
4bSG 139

*T*he man who is truly converted
is taken into the plan of God,
to work for the salvation of his fellow-men.
In his own life he reproduces the character of Christ.
The earnest, disinterested labor of Christ
in behalf of sinners is repeated in his life;
the same fervor and solicitude is revealed in his prayers.

LUH 17 November 1909

*T*he words of Christ encourage parents
to bring their little ones to Jesus.
They may be wayward,
and possess passions like those of humanity,
but this should not deter us from bringing them to Christ.
ST 9 April 1896

*L*et us do as Christ's apostles did;
let us offer prayer for the sick,
for there are many who cannot have
the advantages of our sanitariums.
The Lord will remove infirmities in answer to prayer.
MM 242

To do her work as it should be done
requires talent and skill and patient, thoughtful care.
It calls for self-distrust and earnest prayer.
Let every mother strive
by persevering effort to fulfill her obligations.
Let her bring her little ones to Jesus in the arms of faith,
telling Him her great need,
and asking for wisdom and grace.
CT 128

We no longer mark out a way
nor seek to bring the Lord to our wishes.
If the life of the sick can glorify Him,
we pray that they may live;
nevertheless, not as we will but as He will.

2T 21

*P*ainstaking effort, prayer and faith,
when united with a correct example, will not be fruitless.
Bring your children to God in faith,
and seek to impress their susceptible minds
with a sense of their obligations to their heavenly Father.
RH 6 November 1883

It was by prayer to His Father
that [Jesus] was braced for duty and for trial.
Day by day He followed His round of duty,
seeking to save souls. . . .
And He spent whole nights
in prayer in behalf of the tempted ones.
Mar 85

We should pray that God will shed light
into the darkened mind and comfort the sorrowful heart.
But God answers prayer for those
who place themselves in the channel of His blessings.
While we offer prayer for these sorrowful ones,
we should encourage them
to try to help those more needy than themselves.
MH 256

The greatest blessing that God can give to man
is the spirit of earnest prayer.
All heaven is open before the man of prayer. . . .
The ambassadors of Christ will have power
with the people after they have,
with earnest supplication, come before God.
RH 20 October 1896

*N*ov. 26, at our season of prayer in the morning,
we were led out to pray fervently that God
would especially bless my husband,
and give him a large measure of his Holy Spirit.
The Spirit of God rested upon us,
and we were especially revived and strengthened in the Lord.

RH 27 February 1866

I determined that my efforts
should never cease till these dear souls,
for whom I had so great an interest, yielded to God.
Several entire nights were spent by me in earnest prayer
for those whom I had sought out
and brought together
for the purpose of laboring and praying with them.
1T 33

At every one of our little meetings
I continued to exhort and pray for each one separately,
until every one had yielded to Jesus,
acknowledging the merits of His pardoning love.
Every one was converted to God.

1T 33, 34

At the time when the danger and depression
of the church are greatest,
the little company who are standing in the light
will be sighing and crying for the abominations
that are done in the land.
But more especially will their prayers arise
in behalf of the church because its members
are doing after the manner of the world.

5T 209, 210

Christianity must supply fathers and mothers
for these homeless ones.
The compassion for the widow and the orphan
manifested in prayers and deeds,
will come up in remembrance before God,
to be rewarded by and by.

ChS 215, 216

All night we watched over our child,
earnestly praying
that the disease might be effectually rebuked.
We tried to exercise faith, regardless of appearance,
and our petitions were heard, and the child recovered.
It did seem to us that an angel of God touched him.
2SG 122

$\mathcal{D}$o not expect a change to be wrought
in your children without patient,
earnest labor, mingled with fervent prayer.
To study and understand their varied characters,
and day by day to mould them after the divine Model,
is a work demanding great diligence and perseverance,
and much prayer, with an abiding faith in God's promises.
ST 4 May 1888

It is our work to present the sick and suffering
to Christ in the arms of our faith. . . .
We should lay hold on His promise,
and pray for the manifestation of His power.
The very essence of the gospel is restoration,
and the Saviour would have us bid the sick, the hopeless,
and the afflicted take hold upon His strength.

DA 824, 825

In such cases of affliction,
where Satan has control of the mind,
before engaging in prayer
there should be the closest self-examination
to discover if there are not sins
which need to be repented of, confessed, and forsaken.
Deep humility of soul before God is necessary,
and firm, humble reliance upon the merits
of the blood of Christ alone.

2T 146

The Lord calls for decided efforts
to be put forth in places
where the people know nothing of Bible truth.
Singing and prayer and Bible readings
are needed in the homes of the people.

CT 540

3—P.O.

Often prayer is solicited
for those who are suffering from illness or adversity;
but our prayers are most needed
by the men entrusted with prosperity and influence.
MH 212

*L*et there be much praying
and less talking of the mistakes of others.
By much prayer let self be wholly consecrated to God.
Then work with all the facilities and powers
God has given to help one another
to reach a higher standard.
UL 298

*I*f in one place there are only two or three
who know the truth,
let them form themselves into a band of workers.
Let them keep their bond of union unbroken,
pressing together in love and unity,
encouraging one another to advance,
each gaining courage and strength
from the assistance of the others. . . .
As they work and pray in Christ's name,
their numbers will increase.

7T 21

In praying for the sick,
we are to pray that if it is God's will
that they may be raised to health;
but if not that he will give them his grace to comfort,
his presence to sustain them in their suffering.
GCDB 2 February 1897

The sick will be led to Christ by the patient attention
of nurses who anticipate their wants,
and who bow in prayer
and ask the great Medical Missionary
to look with compassion upon the sufferer
and to let the soothing influence of His grace
be felt and His restoring power be exercised.
MM 191, 192

We have united in earnest prayer
around the sickbed of men, women, and children,
and have felt that they were given back to us
from the dead in answer to our earnest prayers.
CH 378

Three times a day we went alone before God,
and engaged in earnest prayer for the recovery of his health. . . .
Frequently one of us would be prostrated by the power of God.
The Lord graciously heard our earnest cries,
and my husband began to recover. . . .
These seasons of prayer were very precious.
We were brought into a sacred nearness to God,
and had sweet communion with him.

2SG 198, 199

Select another and still another soul,
daily seeking guidance from God,
laying everything before Him in earnest prayer,
and working in divine wisdom.
As you do this,
you will see that God will give the Holy Spirit to convict,
and the power of the truth to convert, the soul.
MM 245

I urge our people to cease their criticism and evil-speaking,
and go to God in earnest prayer,
asking Him to help them to help the erring.
Let them link up with one another and with Christ.
RC 200

$\mathcal{L}$et the Los Angeles church have special
seasons of prayer daily for the work that is being done.
The blessing of the Lord will come to the church members
who thus participate in the work,
gathering in small groups daily to pray for its success.
Thus the believers will obtain grace for themselves,
and the work of the Lord will be advanced.
Ev 111, 112

*B*ear in mind that the success of reproof
depends greatly upon the spirit in which it is given.
Do not neglect earnest prayer
that you may possess a lowly mind,
and that angels of God may go before you
to work upon the hearts you are trying to reach,
and so soften them by heavenly impressions
that your efforts may avail.

2T 53

In calling God our Father,
we recognize all His children as our brethren.
We are all a part of the great web of humanity,
all members of one family.
In our petitions we are to include our neighbors
as well as ourselves.
No one prays aright who seeks a blessing for himself alone.
SD 267

As workers for God
we want more of Jesus and less of self.
We should have more of a burden for souls,
and should pray daily that strength and wisdom
may be given us for the Sabbath.
Teachers, meet with your classes.
Pray with them, and teach them how to pray.
Let the heart be softened,
and the petitions short and simple, but earnest.
CSW 125

It is the duty of Christian parents, morning and evening,
by earnest prayer and persevering faith,
to make a hedge about their children.
They should patiently instruct them—
kindly and untiringly teach them how to live
in order to please God.
CG 519

The Lord's promise, "They shall lay hands on the sick,
and they shall recover" (Mark 16:18),
is just as trustworthy now as in the days of the apostles.
It presents the privilege of God's children,
and our faith should lay hold of all that it embraces.
MH 226

At the sound of fervent prayer,
Satan's whole host trembles.
He continues to call legions of his evil angels
to accomplish his object.
And when angels, all-powerful,
clothed with the armory of heaven,
come to the help of the fainting, pursued soul,
Satan and his host fall back,
well knowing that their battle is lost.
RH 13 May 1862

Many will be called into the field
to labor from house to house,
giving Bible readings
and praying with those who are interested.
9T 172

We prayed earnestly to God for the mother,
following the direction given in James v.
We had the assurance that our prayers were heard.
Jesus was in our midst to break the power of Satan,
and release the captive.
2SG 110

If more prayer were offered in our sanitariums
for the healing of the sick,
the mighty power of the Healer would be seen.
Many more would be strengthened and blessed,
and many more acute sicknesses would be healed.
3SM 295

In praying for the sick, it is essential to have faith;
for it is in accordance with the word of God. . . .
Sometimes answers to our prayers come immediately,
sometimes we have to wait patiently
and continue earnestly to plead for the things we need.
HL 240

Students should have their own seasons of prayer,
where they may offer fervent, simple petitions that God
shall bless the president of the school with physical strength,
mental clearness, moral power, and spiritual discernment,
and that every teacher shall be qualified
by the grace of Christ to do his work.
FE 293

You are linked to our souls as part and parcel of us.
We have held most earnest seasons of prayer in your behalf
and we believe that the Lord has listened to our prayers.
I have felt so anxious about you I could not sleep.

10MR 32

*W*hen the gospel net is cast,
let there be a watching by the net,
with tears and earnest prayer.
Let the workers determine not to become discouraged;
and not to let go the net until it is drawn ashore,
with the fruit of their labor.

ST 16 March 1882

*L*et us strive to bring souls into the light of truth,
by opening to them the Scriptures,
and by praying with them,
and urging them to accept Jesus as their Saviour.
And as you engage in this work, Jesus is your Helper,
even the same Jesus that has passed over the road before us.
PH113 17

The Saviour would have us encourage the sick,
the hopeless, the afflicted, to take hold upon His strength.
Through faith and prayer
the sickroom may be transformed into a Bethel.
MH 226

*H*e will not refuse to hear the parents' earnest prayer,
that is seconded by persevering labor,
that their children may be blessed of him,
and become faithful workers in his cause.
When parents do their duty in God's appointed way,
they may be sure that their requests for his help
in their home work will be granted.

ST 4 May 1888

$\mathcal{L}$et us also pray earnestly
in behalf of those whom we expect to visit,
by living faith bringing them, one by one,
into the presence of God.
ChS 169

*W*ork among the lowly, the poor, and the oppressed.
We should pray for and with the helpless ones
who have not strength of will
to control the appetites that passion has degraded.
Earnest, persevering effort must be made for the salvation
of those in whose hearts an interest is awakened.

6T 84

In Him there is healing balm for every disease,
restoring power for every infirmity.
His disciples in this time are to pray for the sick
as verily as the disciples of old prayed.
MH 226

$\mathcal{T}$oo often we forget that our fellow laborers
are in need of strength and cheer.
In times of special perplexity and burden,
take care to assure them of your interest and sympathy.
While you try to help them by your prayers,
let them know that you do it.
Send along the line God's message to His workers:
"Be strong and of a good courage." Joshua 1:6.
7T 185

*N*ot all are called to personal labor in foreign fields,
but all can do something by their prayers
and their gifts to aid the missionary work.
6T 29

To those who desire prayer for their restoration to health,
it should be made plain that the violation of God's law,
either natural or spiritual, is sin,
and that in order for them to receive His blessing,
sin must be confessed and forsaken.

MH 228

4—P.O.

They did not ask for a blessing for themselves merely;
they were weighted with the burden
for the salvation of souls.
The gospel was to be carried
to the uttermost parts of the earth,
and they claimed the endowment of power
that Christ had promised.
Then it was that the Holy Spirit was poured out,
and thousands were converted in a day.
DA 827

As to praying for the sick,
it is too important a matter to be handled carelessly.
I believe we should take everything to the Lord,
and make known to God
all our weaknesses and specify all our perplexities.
MM 16

There are souls who have lost their courage;
speak to them, pray for them.
There are those who need the bread of life.
Read to them from the Word of God.
There is a soul sickness no balm can reach,
no medicine heal.
Pray for these, and bring them to Jesus Christ.
And in all your work Christ will be present
to make impressions upon human hearts.
WM 71

There is a Saviour who will reveal Himself
in our sanitariums to save those
who will submit themselves to Him.
The suffering ones can unite with you in prayer,
confessing their sin, and receiving pardon.
3SM 296

As missionary nurses care for the sick
and relieve the distress of the poor,
they will find many opportunities to pray with them,
to read to them from God's word,
to speak of the Saviour. . . .
They can bring a ray of hope
into the lives of the defeated and disheartened.
MM 246, 247

*Un*belief was taking possession of your soul,
and the Lord afflicted you
that you might gain a needed experience.
He blessed us in praying for you,
and He blessed you in answer to our prayers.

4T 83

*L*et the members of the church,
as the representatives of Christ,
unite in prayer and loving entreaty
that the offender may be restored.
The Holy Spirit will speak through His servants,
pleading with the wanderer to return to God.
DA 441

I sought to impress upon fathers and mothers
their duty to lead these inexperienced youth
into the path cast up for the ransomed of the Lord.
They now need special care and tenderness
and earnest prayer.
ST 19 January 1882

As our nurses minister patiently
to those who are sick in body and soul,
let them ask God to work for the suffering ones
that they may be led to know Christ,
and let them believe that their prayers will be answered.
In all that is done let the love of Christ be revealed.
MM 192

And as the church members do their part faithfully,
the Lord will lead and guide His chosen ministers,
and strengthen them for their important work.
In much prayer let us all unite in holding up their hands
and in drawing bright beams from the heavenly sanctuary.
9T 134, 135

*B*rethren and sisters,
have you forgotten that your prayers should go out,
like sharp sickles, with the laborers in the great harvest field?
5T 162

*Even the babe in its mother's arms
may dwell as under the shadow of the Almighty
through the faith of the praying mother.*
DA 512

Fathers and mothers,
will you not lay hold of your work with energy,
perseverance, and love?
Sow the precious seed daily,
with earnest prayer that God will water it
with the dews of grace,
and grant you an abundant harvest.
The Son of God died to redeem a sinful, rebellious race.
Shall we shrink from any toil or sacrifice
to save our own dear children?
ST 24 November 1881

If the saints of God with deep humility fast and pray,
their prayers will prevail.
Jesus will commission holy angels to resist Satan,
and he will be driven back,
and his power broken from off the afflicted ones.
4bSG 103

There are those all around you who have woes,
who need words of sympathy, love, and tenderness,
and our humble, pitying prayers.
3T 530

*B*ut if parents would feel that they are never released
from their burden of educating and training
their children for God,
if they would do their work in faith,
cooperating with God by earnest prayer and work,
they would be successful
in bringing their children to the Saviour.
ST 9 April 1896

When we have prayed for the recovery of the sick,
we can work with all the more energy,
thanking God that we have the privilege
of co-operating with Him,
and asking His blessing on the means
which He Himself has provided.
MH 231

The Spirit of the Lord rested upon the people,
and solemn, earnest prayer was offered to God
in behalf of those who were seeking him.

ST 19 October 1876

Solicit prayer for the souls for whom you labor;
present them before the church
as objects for the supplication.
It will be just what the church needs,
to have their minds called from their little, petty difficulties,
to feel a great burden, a personal interest,
for a soul that is ready to perish.
MM 244, 245

The Saviour often left His disciples
for seasons of prayer with His Father.
At these times He poured out His soul
in strong crying and tears for those He had come to save,
and for power and grace to carry out
the great plan of redeeming the world.
His example in prayer Christ desired
should be a lesson to His disciples in all ages.
LUH 17 November 1909

As young men go forth to preach the truth,
you should have seasons of prayer for them.
Pray that God will connect them with Himself
and give them wisdom, grace, and knowledge.
Pray that they may be guarded from the snares of Satan
and kept pure in thought and holy in heart.
5T 162

As they acknowledge the claims of truth,
they place themselves where they can be helped.
They should entreat those who are experienced,
and have faith, to plead
with the mighty Deliverer in their behalf.
4bSG 103

They realized the greatness of their debt to Him.
By earnest, persevering prayer
they obtained the endowment of the Holy Spirit,
and then they went forth,
weighted with the burden of saving souls. . . .
Shall we be less earnest than were the apostles?
AG 219

*G*od is just as willing to restore the sick
to health now as when the Holy Spirit
spoke these words through the psalmist.
And Christ is the same compassionate physician now
that He was during His earthly ministry.
MH 226

When my children have done wrong,
and I have talked with them kindly
and then prayed with them,
I have never found it necessary after that to punish them.
Their hearts would melt in tenderness
before the Holy Spirit that came in answer to prayer.
CG 525

If several should meet together with one accord,
with hearts burdened for perishing souls,
and should offer earnest, fervent prayers,
they would prove effectual.

RH 23 August 1892

In laboring where there are already some in the faith,
the minister should at first seek
not so much to convert unbelievers, as to train
the church-members for acceptable co-operation. . .
When they are prepared to sustain the minister
by their prayers and labors,
greater success will attend his efforts.

ChS 70

$\mathcal{T}$he church all united in earnest prayer for me,
and once more I consecrated myself to the Lord,
and felt willing to be used to his glory.
While praying, the thick darkness that had enveloped me
was scattered, a bright light, like a ball of fire,
came towards me, and as it fell upon me,
my strength was taken away.
I seemed to be in the presence of Jesus and of angels.
2SG 37

How are the faithful servants of Christ employed?
"Praying always with all prayer and supplication in the Spirit,"
praying in the closet, in the family,
in the congregation, everywhere;
"and watching thereunto with all perseverance."
They feel that souls are in peril,
and with earnest, humble faith
they plead the promises of God in their behalf.

5T 190

Aaron and Hur prepared a seat for Moses,
and then both engaged in holding up his weary hands
until the going down of the sun.
These men thus showed to Israel their duty
to sustain Moses in his arduous work
while he should receive the word from God
to speak to them.
2T 107

If we are under infirmities of body,
it is certainly consistent to trust in the Lord,
making supplications to our God in our own case,
and if we feel inclined to ask others
in whom we have confidence to unite with us
in prayer to Jesus who is the Mighty Healer,
help will surely come if we ask in faith.

MM 16

Sin has brought many of them where they are,—
to a state of feebleness of mind and debility of body.
Shall prayer be offered to the God of heaven
for his healing to come upon them,
then and there, without specifying any condition?
I say, No, decidedly no.
What then shall be done?
Present their cases before Him
who knows every individual by name.

GCDB 26 February 1897

5—P.O.

*H*ow can we honor God,
how can we vindicate his word,
unless we are much in prayer,
appealing to him to manifest his power
in behalf of the perishing?
RH 23 August 1892

Praying for the sick is a most solemn thing,
and we should not enter upon this work
in any careless, hasty way. . . .
When wrongs have been confessed,
the subjects for prayer may be presented
before God in earnestness and faith,
as the Spirit of God may move upon you.
GCDB 2 February 1897

*L*et every sincere Christian
who has a connection with our schools,
be determined to be a faithful servant in the cause of Christ. . . .
Every day they may exert a silent, prayerful influence,
and co-operate with Jesus Christ,
the missionary-in-chief to our world.

FE 293

It has often been my privilege to pray with the sick.
We should do this much more often than we do.
3SM 295

I felt the spirit of prayer.
We prayed to the Lord to deliver the afflicted.
In the name and strength of Jesus
I put my arms around her, and lifted her up from the bed,
and rebuked the power of Satan, and bid her,
"Go free." She was instantly brought out of the fit,
and praised the Lord with us.
We had a solemn, refreshing season in this place.

2SG 71

$\mathcal{D}$o you feel that your prayers are unanswered?
Then do as Christ directs you. . . .
Will you work in behalf of the oppressed?
Will you practice the life of Christ
in seeking to save the souls ready to perish?
In such work you will have the comfort
of the grace of God in rich measure.
1SAT 351

All that we are required to do is to ask God
to raise the sick up if in accordance with His will,
believing that He hears the reasons which we present
and the fervent prayers offered.
If the Lord sees it will best honor Him,
He will answer our prayers.
But to urge recovery without submission
to His will is not right.
2T 147, 148

*W*hile Jerusalem was hushed in silence,
and the disciples had returned to their homes
to obtain refreshment in sleep, Jesus slept not.
His divine pleadings were ascending
to his Father for his disciples,
that they might be kept from the evil influences
which they would daily encounter in the world,
and that his own soul might be strengthened and braced
for the duties and trials of the coming day.

RH 17 August 1886

$\mathcal{J}$esus pleaded, not for one only,
but for all His disciples:
"Father, I will that they also whom thou hast given me,
be with me where I am" (John 17:24). . . .
He felt the burdens and sorrows of every tempest-tossed soul,
and that earnest prayer included . . .
all His followers to the close of time.
LHU 175

After you have done your duty faithfully to your children,
then carry them to God and ask Him to help you.
Tell Him that you have done your part,
and then in faith ask God to do His part,
that which you cannot do.
CG 256

With joy unutterable, parents see the crown,
the robe, the harp, given to their children.
The days of hope and fear are ended.
The seed sown with tears and prayers
may have seemed to be sown in vain,
but their harvest is reaped with joy at last.
Their children have been redeemed.
CG 569

KEY TO ABBREVIATED TITLES

1SAT	*Sermons and Talks*, volume 1
1T, 2T, etc.	*Testimonies for the Church* (9 volumes)
2SG, 4bSG	*Spiritual Gifts,* volumes 2, 4b
3BC	*Seventh-day Adventist Bible Commentary,* volume 3
3SM	*Selected Messages,* book 3
6MR, 10MR, 21MR	*Manuscript Releases,* volumes 6, 10, 21
AG	*God's Amazing Grace*
CG	*Child Guidance*
CH	*Counsels on Health*
COL	*Christ's Object Lessons*
CSW	*Counsels on Sabbath School Work*
CT	*Counsels to Parents, Teachers, and Students*
DA	*The Desire of Ages*

Ev	*Evangelism*
FE	*Fundamentals of Christian Education*
GCDB	*General Conference Daily Bulletin*
GosHealth	*The Gospel of Health*
GW	*Gospel Workers*
HL	*Healthful Living*
HP	*In Heavenly Places*
LHU	*Lift Him Up*
LUH	*Lake Union Herald*
Mar	*Maranatha*
MH	*The Ministry of Healing*
MM	*Medical Ministry*
MYP	*Messages to Young People*
PC	*Paulson Collection of Ellen G. White Letters*
PH113	*Words of Encouragement to Self-supporting Workers*
RC	*Reflecting Christ*

RH	*The Advent Review and Sabbath Herald*
SD	*Sons and Daughters of God*
ST	*Signs of the Times*
TDG	*This Day With God*
TM	*Testimonies to Ministers and Gospel Workers*
UL	*The Upward Look*
WM	*Welfare Ministry*

If you enjoyed this quote book on prayer, consider the other topical books in this series:

Angels
Assurance
Comfort
Joy
Peace